For Gurbani, my sunflower.

ISBN: 978-1-913339-66-1
Text copyright © Monika Singh Gangotra 2021
Illustrations copyright © Michaela Dias-Hayes 2021

A catalogue record of this book is available from the British Library.
No part of this publication may be reproduced, stored in a
retrieval system or transmitted in any form or by any means
without prior permission from the author. All rights reserved.

SUNFLOWER SISTERS

MONIKA SINGH GANGOTRA

MICHAELA DIAS-HAYES

First published in the UK
2021 by Owlet Press
www.owletpress.com

"*I see wedding preparations have begun,*" said Mr Jones from next door.
"*Yes!*" squealed Amrita, helping Dad hang the lights.
"*My brother Yemi's getting married too,*" Kiki said, grinning.

"*It's so bright today,*" chirped Ms Laurette.
"*Would you girls like sun cream? We don't want your beautiful skin to burn.*"
"*Yes please,*" the girls replied politely.
"*Oh, look! Our guests have arrived,*" Amrita's dad
said as a taxi pulled up. "*There's still lots to do!*"

Aunty hugged Amrita with a tight squeeze.
"My, how you've grown!" she smiled. *"Now, come on in out of the sun – you don't want to get a tan before the wedding!"*

Dad shook his head and sent the girls inside.

"*Jas! What is that on your face?*" yelled Amrita. Mum was not pleased at all. "*Aunty brought this cream over for me, to make my skin look fair and bright for the wedding,*" said Jas, looking unsure.

"*Eww! What if Shahid doesn't recognise you?*" Amrita and Kiki laughed. "*Don't tease your sister, Amrita,*" Aunty said, frowning. "*Jas needs to look her absolute best for her big day! You'll miss her when she is married and moved out. Besides, maybe you should try…*"

"Oh stop, Aunty!" snapped Mum. She took Jas's hand and lovingly wiped the cream off her face. "Your skin is lovely, just as it is, my precious daughter. Tomorrow you'll be the most beautiful bride anyone's ever seen."

"I have to go home now," Kiki said, giving Amrita a goodbye hug. "Here, take some sweets and be sure to give our blessings to your brother and family, Kiki," said Mum. "We hope you all have a wonderful celebration tomorrow." She turned to Amrita … "It's time for your bath, Beta. Come on, up those stairs."

"Here let me help, Amrita," said Daddi. "We'll have you sparkling as white as snowdrops for the wedding tomorrow."

"EEK! Daddi! Stop – that tickles!" Amrita giggled.
"Snowdrops?" gasped Mum, creating a whirlpool in the bath water. *"No! I prefer golden-brown autumn leaves swirling and whirling in the breeze!"*

As Amrita got ready for a cup of masala chai after her bath,
Daddi gave her a loving squeeze.

"Yes, you really are beautiful like the leaves in autumn.

Do you know people travel from miles around to see the browns and golds of the changing leaves? It's a marvel, just like you."

"Don't let Amrita drink too much tea," Aunty said with a grumpy grimace. "And we told you every day, when you were pregnant with Amrita, to drink saffron and milk, but did you listen…"

"Oh Aunty, not this nonsense again!" said Dad, rolling his eyes.
"Come on, Amrita. Time for bed."

"Why shouldn't I drink too much tea?" asked Amrita.
"It's silly old wives' tales, my darling. For years, people would eat or avoid certain foods. They'd wear smelly creams or stay out of the sun, thinking it would make their skin lighter and that this was more beautiful than having darker skin."

Amrita wrinkled her nose. *"That's ridiculous."*

"I know, Beta. It's nonsense."
Mum sighed and gave Amrita a goodnight kiss.
"We need to teach them that the skin we are in is EXACTLY as it is meant to be."

The big day arrived. *"Look at all these beautiful colours, Amrita,"* Mum smiled. *"Which one would you like to wear?"* Amrita clapped her hands in delight.

"I want to look just like the sunflower in our garden," Amrita said with a big smile. *"It's so pretty and just as tall as me. So … yellow, please!"*

"YELLOW?!" gasped Aunty, entering the room. "With YOUR complexion?"

"I have just the outfit for you, Amrita," whispered Mum. "Follow me. I've been saving this for just the right moment…"

"My mother gave it to me when I was your age," Mum revealed as Amrita grabbed the box.
"Mum, why was Aunty surprised when I chose yellow?" Amrita asked.

"Well, some people think that wearing certain colours makes our skin look darker," Mum said.

"But shouldn't we wear colours that make us happy?" Amrita replied. "Our skin is beautiful, whatever colour we wear, right?"

"That's right, Amrita," Mum said. "When I wore this outfit, my mum said I reminded her of the sun — warm and kind. Yellow has been my favourite colour EVER since."

"*Do I look like the sun too?*" asked Amrita.
"*You look even more beautiful, just like the tall sunflowers, proud and radiant,*" Mum said, beaming with pride.

"*Then I will always look up towards you, because you are my sun,*" Amrita replied, holding Mum's hand tightly.

The wedding was wonderful! Amrita felt AMAZING in her yellow lehenga.

After the ceremony, as Jas was saying goodbye to her family,
Amrita twirled like a sunflower spinning towards the sunshine.

She wanted to remember this
happy feeling as she closed her eyes,
enjoying the warmth on her face.

Aunty watched Amrita dancing. *"She looks so beautiful in that outfit and I am sure your mum would have been so happy to see her wearing it today,"* she whispered to Amrita's mum.

Amrita's mum looked towards the sun with a teary smile.

Just then, Amrita heard something…

Music! Another family was celebrating a wedding on the other side of the street. Amrita's eyes opened wide as she looked a little closer and spotted something.

Another little sunflower with a beautiful face, looking up at the sun…

Standing in a sea of yellow and the boldest blue ... was Kiki!

Amrita grabbed Mum's hand and pulled her across the road.

Kiki and her mum let Amrita peek inside to see waves of yellow, gold and blue twirling around the dance floor.

Everyone cheered and sang as Yemi and his bride were showered with money while they began to dance. This was a day that Amrita and Kiki would never forget.

Outside, their mums smiled at each other knowingly as Kiki and Amrita made one another a promise.

"Sunflower Sisters!"

They both laughed as they locked fingers and then gave each other the biggest hug.

From that moment on, the girls would make sure they felt like sunflowers every day.

And they never broke their promise…

...EVER!

WHAT IS COLOURISM?

Colourism is when people are treated differently because of the shade, tone and colour of their skin. People may be seen as more beautiful or of a higher class because they have lighter coloured skin, compared to other people in their own community who have darker skin. This often happens between people within their own race, but this bias can also come from people of another race too. A lot of history has contributed to what our world sees as beautiful.

WHY IS THIS BAD?

Unfortunately, some people (including family members) can think in this way. This can make darker-skinned people very sad. They might even try to make their skin lighter (sometimes in very dangerous ways) just to try and fit in: using harmful skin-lightening creams, having surgical treatment and eating or avoiding certain foods. Some people don't even play in the sunshine, thinking it will make their skin darker! It is our job as grown ups, and your job too, to help them see why this is wrong. The best way to do this is with learning and kindness. The more information you have, the better equipped you are to make things change around you.

WHAT CAN WE DO TO CHANGE THIS?

Talk, listen and learn about colourism. If you want more information, ask a grown-up if they can help. You might be little people, but you have big voices. Speak to your friends, teachers, siblings and grown-ups about colourism. If you see or hear anything that doesn't sound like kindness about another person's skin colour, use your brave voice to tell them that all the shades of the skin colour rainbow are beautiful.

Love yourself. When you look in the mirror every morning, after brushing your teeth, say to yourself, "I AM UNIQUE AND THAT MAKES ME BEAUTIFUL!"

We think your skin is beautiful and that you are awesome, just the way you are!

And most importantly, be someone's sunflower!
Loving one another for who we are is a great way to change the world!